What Does It Mean to Be GREEN?

Words by Rana DiOrio
Pictures by Addy Rivera Sonda

Little Pickle Press

What does it mean to be green?

Does it mean being good with plants? No.

Does it mean feeling sick in the car? No.

Does it mean looking like a frog,
or a pickle, or an alien? No!

Being green means...

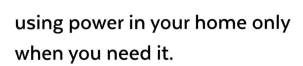

using power in your home only
when you need it.

...eating foods grown locally, or even from your own garden.

...walking or rolling to the park instead of getting a ride in a car.

...packing your lunch and drink in containers you bring home every day.

...enjoying your ice cream in a cone, rather than in a paper cup with a plastic spoon.

...picking up trash that isn't yours and putting it in the garbage.

...putting bottles, cans, plastic, and paper into recycling bins.

...composting food scraps to fertilize your garden.

...collecting and using rainwater instead of water from the tap.

WATER MELON

COMPOST DIRT

...drawing on two sides of your paper instead of just one,

then repurposing your artwork
to make other creations.

...wearing your pajamas one more time before washing them.

...turning off the water while you wash your hands or brush your teeth.

...reimagining the systems that affect our earth most—water, waste, energy, and fuel.

WAVE ENERGY

Buoy

Tether

Pump

Attachment
and Foundation

WIND ENERGY

1. Kite pulls the tether outwards.

2. This rotates the generator, producing electricity.

3. Once tether reaches its end, a small amount of power is lost as the kite is retracted and the cycle starts again.

4. A second kite on each generator rotates in an opposing cycle to ensure a constant process.

Tether

Generator

...understanding that we depend on Mother Earth and she depends on us.

So spread the word about being green—if we work together,
we can live in harmony with our planet!

Being Green

I was seven years old when Little Pickle Press published the first edition of my mom's book *What Does It Mean to Be Green?* Climate science has changed *a lot* since then. I will not lie to you—the environmental crisis is becoming increasingly alarming in myriad ways. In the time between this book's initial release and February 2021, approximately 160 species have gone extinct, over 17 trillion gallons of water have been wasted (that's enough to fill close to 26 million Olympic-size swimming pools), and five of the warmest years on Earth since 1880 have occurred (as a result of climate change). This is just the tip of the iceberg—oh yeah, and the glaciers are melting too. But this does not mean that we should give up hope. Instead, it is a call to action. If each and every one of us can commit to being just a little more environmentally conscientious ("green") each and every day, well, we might actually have a shot at saving this magnificent planet we call home.

—Ryan Stretch, St. Ignatius College Prep, Class of 2022

"I've learned you are never too small to make a difference."

—Greta Thunberg, in her speech at the UN COP24 Climate Talks in 2018

"Mother Earth is hurting. And she needs a generation of thoughtful, caring, and active kids like all of you to protect her for the future."

—Leonardo DiCaprio, Academy Award-winning actor and environmental champion

"What you do makes a difference, and you have to decide what kind of difference you want to make."

—Dr. Jane Goodall, scientist & activist

What You Can Do

You have so much power when it comes to promoting sustainability. To start, lead by example by following the five *R*s of zero-waste living!

- **Refuse:** Say no to what you don't need.
- **Reduce:** Use less. Donate or sell what you no longer need.
- **Reuse:** Switch disposable items for reusable alternatives. Find new ways to use your old things.
- **Recycle:** Sort your waste correctly and minimize what you send to the landfill.
- **Rot**: Compost your household waste or participate in a composting program for organic waste.

Here are a few things you, your family, and friends can do to be green by practicing the five *R*s (remember to ask for the help of a caring adult when you are unsure):

Refuse
- The straw or plastic cutlery that's offered and use your reusable straw and kitchen utensils instead.
- The plastic bottle of water that's offered and drink from your own water bottle instead.

Reduce
- Donate or sell the clothes that no longer fit you.
- Give the books you no longer read to someone who will.

Reuse
- Use a dish towel instead of paper towels.
- Ask a caring adult to turn your too-short jeans into cut-offs.

Recycle
- Choose food items that are packaged in recyclable (or even better, biodegradable/compostable) materials.
- Buy products and clothes made from recycled materials, then recycle them when you are finished with them.

Rot
- Learn the rules of composting at home—skins of fruits and vegetables, tea bags, coffee grounds, eggshells, flowers, hair(!), etc.
- Volunteer at a cooperative organic (maybe even a school or urban) garden and learn how to use compost to fertilize soil.

About the Author

RANA DIORIO grew up in Rhode Island, went to college in North Carolina, and attended law school in Tennessee. It wasn't until she moved to California's environmentally conscious Bay Area, however, that she started developing her own appreciation of what it means to be green. She realized that we all have the power to change the way we live to be respectful of, and grateful for, Mother Earth and to help her thrive. Rana has written her way through life—as a student, lawyer, investment banker, investor, and now as an author and entrepreneur. Her interests include fitness training; practicing yoga; reading nonfiction and children's books; dreaming; walking along beaches; effecting positive change; and, of course, being global, green, present, safe, kind, entrepreneurial, and American, like the other books in her What Does It Mean to Be...?® series.

About the Illustrator

ADDY RIVERA SONDA is a Mexican illustrator who loves color, learning, and exploring ways in which we could build a kinder and more sustainable world. Her biggest inspiration for drawing is that she knows that stories and art are slowly but surely changing the way people understand themselves and perceive others, building empathy, and a more inclusive world.

To Paula, for her courage, strength, and grace...and for loving me just the way I am.

—RD

To every kid who dares to imagine a kinder world for everyone. Imagination is the first step for creation.

—ARS

Published by Little Pickle Press, an imprint of Sourcebooks eXplore

P.O. Box 4410, Naperville, Illinois 60567-4410

(630) 961-3900

sourcebookskids.com

Library of Congress Cataloging-in-Publication Data is on file with the publisher.

Source of Production: Leo Paper, Heshan City, Guangdong Province, China

Date of Production: April 2021

Run Number: 5021485

Printed and bound in China.

LEO 10 9 8 7 6 5 4 3 2 1

Discover more
of the award-winning
What Does It Mean to Be...?® series